Little People, **BIG DREAMS™**

BILLIE JEAN KING

Written by
Maria Isabel Sánchez Vegara

Illustrated by
Miranda Sofroniou

Frances Lincoln
Children's Books

Billie Jean was a little girl born on the sunny coast of California. Her family loved all kinds of sports, and her dad always encouraged her and her brother to run after any ball.

The game she liked most was baseball. She even thought of becoming a professional player.

But during her first baseball game, she realized she was the only girl on the field. And there was no place for her past the kids' teams.

She tried many sports until she discovered tennis. It was love at first serve! Her favorite things were running and hitting a ball—and tennis had both.

Best of all: girls and boys
could play together.

Billie Jean did lots of gardening and housework to save enough money to buy her first tennis racket. When she finally held it in her hands, she felt like a champion.

1931
MARYL

She asked her mom to drive her to a court
in the city where a professional tennis player was
giving free lessons. He became her first coach, and
she became his best pupil ever.

After her first lesson, Billie Jean knew
what she wanted to do in life.

Tennis taught her to play by the rules, to know what it feels like to win and lose, and to be a better person.

One day, at a tournament, Billie Jean was pushed aside from a team picture because she was wearing shorts, not a skirt.

That was the dumbest reason not to be in a picture she had ever heard! But that wasn't all...

There were no sports scholarships for girls in college, and women received smaller prizes than men for winning the same tournaments. The higher Billie Jean climbed in tennis, the more she realized her biggest battle would be off the court.

She founded the Women's Tennis Association with eight other bold tennis players.

They all shared a dream: to achieve equal pay
and opportunities for men and women in sports.

In one single season, Billie Jean won three Grand Slams, the most important tournaments in the world. She became the first tennis player and the first woman ever to be named Sportsperson of the Year.

She was so famous that Bobby Riggs, a windbag tennis champion, challenged her to a match called the "Battle of the Sexes."

He thought it would be easy to win against a woman.
But Billie Jean showed him who the real champion was!

WTT

Billie Jean wanted to make tennis a team sport, not a battle. Together with her first husband, Larry, and with the support of Ilana, her later partner, she helped start a new league where all kids would play together.

The day the first sports scholarships were given to women, Billie Jean felt happier than she had lifting any trophy. She was not just a world tennis champion—but the little girl who dreamed of changing things and did.

BILLIE JEAN KING

(Born 1943)

Billie Jean Moffitt was born in Long Beach, California, to a family of athletes. Surrounded by sports from a young age, she soon discovered tennis. She saved money to buy her first tennis racket. Eight dollars later, Billie Jean was ready to play. She took free lessons from professional Clyde Walker and decided that, one day, she would be World No. 1. Billie Jean won her first championship at 15 and turned professional a year later. She was half of the youngest pair to win the Wimbledon women's doubles, and later, won the women's singles championship—becoming a star around the world. With speed, strength, and skill, Billie Jean won match after match to become World No. 1 in women's tennis. But tennis was sometimes unfair: men would receive thousands

of dollars more than women for winning the same tournaments. Along with eight other female players, Billie Jean fought this with a stunt—they would take only one dollar to play tennis! She also founded the Women's Tennis Association to make sure women athletes got a fair deal. Her victory against Bobby Riggs in the "Battle of the Sexes" went down in history as the match that changed tennis. During her career, Billie Jean's tennis partner, Ilana Kloss, became her life partner too. Together, they promote mixed-gender team tennis. In 2009, Billie Jean was awarded the Presidential Medal of Freedom for standing up for gender equality and LGBTQ rights. She is recognized as one of tennis's most exciting players, and a champion on—and off—the court.

Want to find out more about **Billie Jean King?**

Read one of these great books:

Women in Sports: Fifty Fearless Athletes Who Played to Win by Rachel Ignotofsky

I Am Billie Jean King by Brad Meltzer and Christopher Eliopoulos

Original idea of the series by Maria Isabel Sánchez Vegara, published by Alba Editorial, S.L.U.
"Little People, BIG DREAMS" and "Pequeña & Grande" are trademarks of
Alba Editorial S.L.U. and/or Beautifool Couple S.L.
First published in the US in 2020 by Frances Lincoln Children's Books, an imprint of The Quarto Group.
100 Cummings Center, Suite 265D, Beverly, MA 01915, USA, Tel: +1 978-282-9590 **www.Quarto.com**
First Published in Spain in 2020 under the title Pequeña & Grande Billie Jean King
by Alba Editorial, S.L.U., Baixada de Sant Miquel, 1, 08002 Barcelona, Spain www.albaeditorial.es

Published by arrangement with Alba Editorial, S.L.U. Translation rights arranged by IMC Agència Literària, SL

A CIP record for this book is available from the Library of Congress.
ISBN 978-0-7112-4693-5
eISBN 978-0-7112-5493-0
Set in Futura BT.
Published by Katie Cotton · Designed by Karissa Santos
Edited by Rachel Williams and Katy Flint · Production by Caragh McAleenan
Manufactured in Shanghai, China CC092023
9 7 5 4 6 8

Photographic acknowledgments (pages 28–29, from left to right) 1. Photo taken of Billie Jean King, April 1958 via New-York Historical Society. 2. Billie-Jean's Win, 1966 © Keystone / Stringer via Getty Images 3. Original 9, 1970 via WTA. 4. Obama Honors Sixteen With Congressional Medal Of Freedom, 2009 © Chip Somodevilla / Staff via Getty Images.

Collect the *Little People*, **BIG DREAMS**™ series:

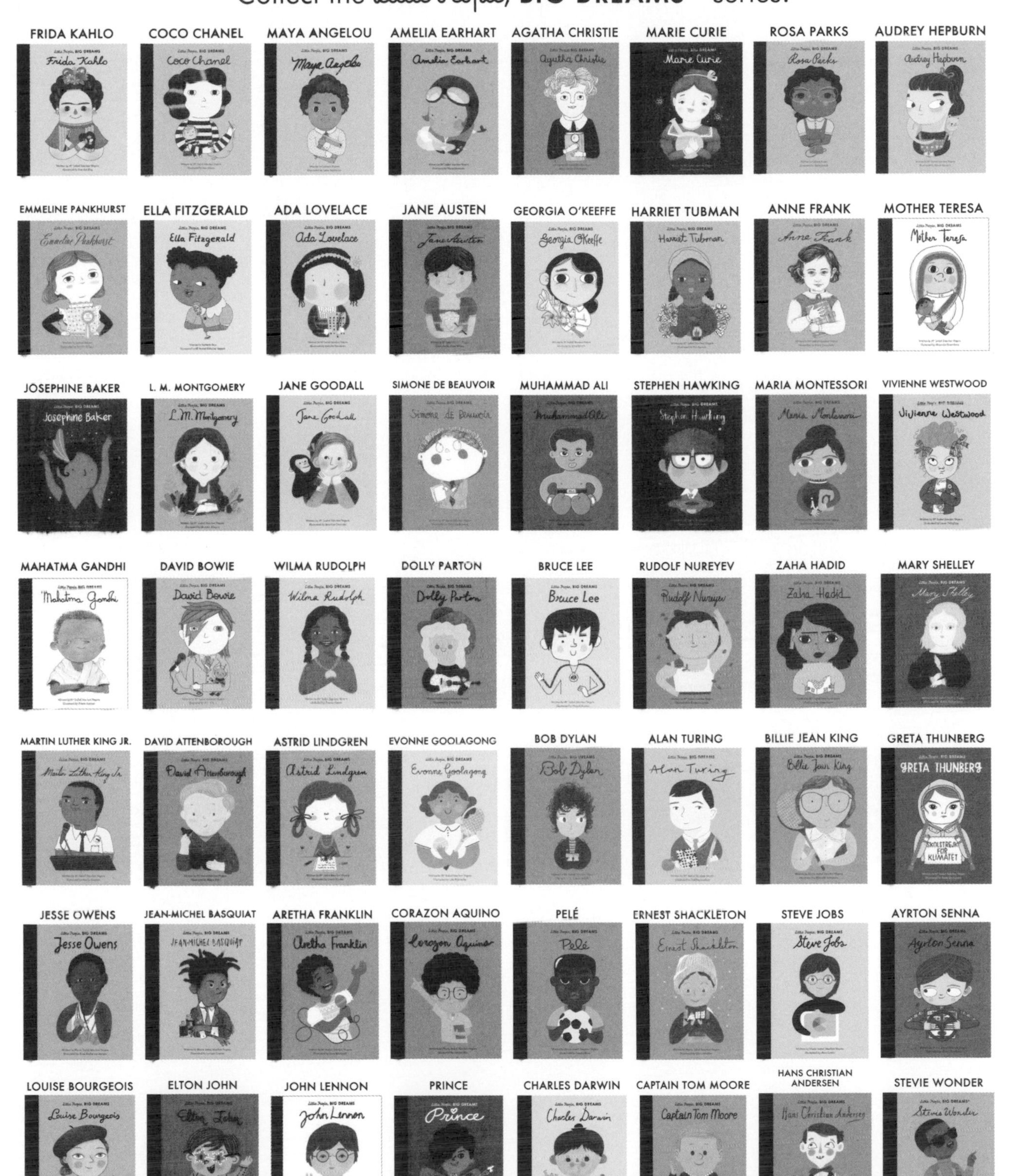

Scan the QR code for free activity sheets, teachers' notes and more information about the series at www.littlepeoplebigdreams.com